Ashes Where the Hurt Was

Addreonna Seger

BookLeaf Publishing

India | USA | UK

Presentation by *BookLeaf Publishing*

Web: www.bookleafpub.com

E-mail: info@bookleafpub.com

ISBN: 9789358310191

First edition 2023

Ani,

Thank you for pulling me out of my comfort zone and into this wild (scary?) world all while holding my hand. You are seriously my best friend and I am so happy to have you in my life. This one is for you- for believing in me, for never letting me give up on myself, for your patience through the writing and editing processes, and especially, for encouraging me to follow my dreams. For all the stories we share and all the stories we have left to tell; I love you all the bioluminescent algae.

ACKNOWLEDGEMENT

Oh boy, where do I even start? I have so many people I'm grateful for and to. I guess I'll just dive in.

Dad- For inspiring my love for poetry specifically. Without you (and those painfully beautiful Edgar Allan Poe anthologies), none of this would have ever been a reality.

Mom- I will forever appreciate you for fostering my love of reading from such an early age.

Luc, Brayden, and CJ- They say nobody teaches you like your own children. I don't pretend to know who "they" are or why they know all this stuff- but facts are facts. My children have taught me so much and given me so much hope for life. You guys are incredible and I love you!

Fanceey- For never letting me wallow and always calling me on my bullshit. I need that! But also, thank you immensely for always sticking by my side and being the best sister in the world. All of your support, love, and efforts are so appreciated and I can't even begin to tell you all that you mean to me. I don't have enough space!

Madeline- For always holding space for me and listening to my squirrel-y thoughts and encouraging me to have fun with language 'cause "Shakespeare made up words all the time!"

Tania- For never letting me give up while reminding me how important rest,self-care, and self-love truly are.

Mrs. Shackelford, Dr. Crenshaw, Ms. Smith, Mrs. Phillips-Taylor, and Mr. Brady- I did the thing! And I could not have done any of it without some very fantastic guidance. I carry all that you've taught me with me every day. I cannot thank you all enough.

To all the women who've come before me, who've paved the way, who've bled their hearts onto paper- thank you.

Thank you all, from the bottom of my heart.

PREFACE

"Can you understand? Someone, somewhere, can you understand me a little, love me a little? For all my despair, for all my ideals, for all that – I love life. But it is hard, and I have so much – so very much to learn."

— Sylvia Plath, The Journals of Sylvia Plath

A(Side)

I am a (parenthetical girl)
in a hypothetical world.
I focus on worst case
best case scenarios
In my spare time,
I wring the sanity out
of my own mind.
Only to remind myself that
I'm fine.
I'm fine. I'm okay. I'm fine.
I'm fine.
Really; I promise this time.

I'm a walking {s t o p sign.}

and you never deserved me

I am fascinated, watching you
flit around with your
hummingbird heart.
You're navigating blindly,
angrily asking why I won't follow as you
fall over your own laces.
Still, I'm the girl who keeps bending over
backwards
tying and retying them;
double knotting up your insecurities
but baby, I'm running out of string.
You're singing to me again,
burn the bridge, fall in the river.
Find your center, don't panic,
let the currents carry you.
And it took me a long time to realize
the river was my tears
and the currents were your misery.
Everything we ever had was built
on my accepting misery as a paradigm
and how well I handled it (or didn't);
the precarious situation I found myself
drowning in-

Hymns of Hope

9

I am a bomb shelter underground
in a war zone.
I am a metal cage
when the sharks smell blood
I am a warrior with a
shield and sword.

I will always stand
by your side.
I will always protect you.

Subconcious Delusions

Codependent Cinderella
are you so addicted to
the saccharine that you've
forgotten what happens when
happy ever after falls apart?

Does it ever feel lonely
being the only
one still hopelessly clinging
to the fairytale of your youth?

'Cause I saw our
utopian imaginations
destroyed, one by one.
And I saw the promises of my
generation go unrealized.

Again and again,
I've mourned the fables.

A hazy dream
in forest of surreal trees,
walks me further into the fantasy.
Down, down, down into the
darkness of the dreamscape,

where I very gently
let go of the trivial.
But I never could control
the sadness
or the contradictions.
                    (why is it always

midnight?)

Ghosting

My will falls
around my feet,
bunched like a
crumpled cocktail dress.
I accept my defeat.

Passion melts my cool girl mask;
I am impatiently loving through
all my fears that I keep
pretending aren't true.

Catch a ride, enjoy the drive
scream into the void- realign.
Catch a body, caught a vibe
(and some feelings I plan to deny.)

Precious, I, cared
by mistake.

It was an accident.
Anything to justify;
take the shame off
(of feeling too fast)
of falling too fast.

Oh, the unrequited
loneliness.

Animal

The memories we create
are embedded under my skin.
A bouquet of burst capillaries
Lingering fingers lightly trace
bruises from last night; a
whisper of our sins.

Whiskey on our breath,
sharp bright drips
you can taste on my tongue.
I can feel my neurons
pulling my body to yours.
Synapse ticking like Morse code.
Primal and ravenous;
we eat each other alive.

Hiding

Tell me what you
think you've learned
becoming somebody else.

Strangers pulling strings
to move your mouth,
their
fingers tickling you
from the inside
out.

Does your brain scream?

Tell me what you think
you know about growing up.
Dead end life at a dead end
job and a boss with things
to oversee;
domestic and domesticated.

Strings, puppet.
A whore.
And more strings.

Tell me what you know about

better, or worse.
The flood of a river you sank in
is dried and cracked along the banks
aching for the rain to bring relief.

Go ahead and tell me what
you learned about becoming
different (better than me).
So I can tell them
what I know
you're hiding.

Quiet Love

i'm simply not the girl willing
to stand outside your glass walls
(i'm done with hoops)
i won't perform in your circus or
pantomime my love for you;

i stand statue still and
stare into the glass,
met with my own eyes, i wonder
can you see me? Are you staring back?

i am also no longer the girl who
screams her vocal cords
black and blue; so now

you can be still and listen to me
as i whisper
if you ever get tired of looking
at me through your sad windows.

Modern Day Romance

I told him his angel number
was three
And he asked me
"what does that mean?"

I sent him a link.
He seemed shocked.
Asked me if "shook"
was the right word.

Numbers are patterns;
the language of the universe.
Fibonacci hidden in the flowers
and along all the spirals
leading to everything and nothing.

Mathematically, all that means is:
                        he's my golden ratio.

Idk, I'm Impulsive!

Thought you was heaven sent,
You gave me all your promises
and I believed every little bit.
Unlocked the gate, opened my door
let you in and
you tracked mud all over my floors.

But I cleaned up the mess;
cleaning up mess is what I do best.

You stayed for a little while;
got comfortable being
with someone
who gave you peace,
and a slower pace,
and a place to rest.

The problem,
my ungracious guest,
my antagonizing regret,
my biggest heartbreak,

is that you're so
uncomfortable with yourself
you prefer chaos,

you prefer speed,
you prefer not to sleep.

You want what you want
And I'm not sure of the moral
of the story anymore.

I was "inadequate"
but honestly
she just left for the hell of it.

Mushroom Clouds

I,
am leaden and magnetic.
A bomb shelter for broken men.
They are radioactive,
erosive bio-hazards;
rust me out from my center.

Still,
we pulled it together
even as the chemical reactions
rotted the earth beneath our feet
until we fell into a living hell.

Couldn't escape;
or save anyone.
I stayed put, properly,
until it was "me" or "them."

Pulled myself out
of ground zero grasping the
hanging roots and
broken
water mains until I could
see the blue skies
littered with little mushroom
clouds.

Online Interactions Not Rated™

I don't even remember what you said.
Maybe it was Memphis?
I am casually fascinated by you.
We're talking about nothing
and I'm completely wrapped up in it.

The conversation flows and I find
myself paying more attention to
what you're saying than the
aggro of the entire village
I have distractedly pulled.

(Thank god I'm a tank.) Anyway-
I do not look forward to you, yet.
But I do not ignore the feeling
I felt nonetheless.

So distracted.

I've definitely walked
aimlessly around this camp
about five or six times now.

I might be in trouble.

Overdose

I'm an overdose.
The high is good
for a while
Until the panic sets in
"Maybe," you think
"I've had too much."
And that heartbeat
hammering your ribs
isn't love, darling.
And that's why you're
sweating
And that's why it's
hard to breathe.
Try not to
succumb to sleep
you might lose
    everything.

eXX/eXY

You know,
>I admit
I'm a
>bit of
a pragmatist
>in relationships
I just,
>you know,
if it's
>not broken
then why
>fix it?
Balance, all
>things equitable
from one
>side to
the other.
>The divine
double eX
>helix and
the comedy
>of the
eX solving
>for Y.

Clean Break

Fractured
   Fairytale, I   believe
       in   you.
 Why
            don't you
        believe
          in
     me
   too?

Withdrawl

"In case of emergency,"
it said, break the glass.
Behind the glass sat a
blood red axe.

My bloodstained memory abstracts
a fragmented shattering until
the picture sharpens like
so much broken glass.

Tell me, my love,
how you breathe so dead inside?

I put my fist through the glass
and the blood red axe
is just in reach.
The broken glass is reminiscent
of your shattered pieces
spread out, vast as any ocean;
uncharted territory,
the gasping breaths in the murky depths;
you keep your secrets to yourself.

The bathroom door is locked so I swing the axe
until the hinges break free.

I violently gag as I try to drag you out;
the visions of your limp body
wading in bile on the tile of my floor.
I pull you away with my free hand
covering my mouth and nose with
the other as the flames devour the room

The smoke and heat burn my eyes
my tears are stinging; self-preservation
kicks in at the threshold.
I can't keep saving you from yourself,
it's an exercise in futility and it's going to kill
me.
Your selfish disease is all consuming,
takes your life and the breath out of me.
I can't do this anymore.

So, there's broken glass and
bloody knuckles and an addict checked out
on the welcome mat.
I ran until my feet bled; I ran away
until the alarm wailing in the distance
screamed itself silent;
until my memory goes black.

Broken Code

The words stick to your skin
like barbed wire.
And they penetrate much
further in.
Infect your bloodstream
send the words that don't even
belong to you, to your brain.

And you rewire and rewrite
your own coding by trusting in
someone else's

        error codes.
"<b>Broken;" codes;
[alternative

      / splicing.]
Codes missing depth and nuance.
Codes machines can't follow.
Get it?
Machines can't follow.

You are flawed; it is
human & beautiful.

Coffee & Cinnamon Rolls (In the Morning)

She stood at the kitchen sink;
washing the vegetables
from the garden
She's always so gorgeous
when she tends
the harvest.
Her clothes covered
in dirt; her gray hair
thrown up into a bun.

He stood at their
kitchen island
with his hands spread
at length.
He's quiet; awe-struck
at this woman;
his heart skipped a beat
as she shifted her feet.

She clears her throat
"You know I heard your
knees creakin' when you
walked in the door;
come here stranger."

He walks slowly toward her
"damn these old bones"
and kisses her like it's
the very first and last
they'll ever have.

They've been doing
this for half a century.
Her hearing him
sneaking up,
him rolling his eyes.

He always said
you couldn't sneak up
on a woman like that.
But she sure
snuck up on him.

Half a century gone and
they have created
such a beautiful life.
And they still have
dinners by candlelight
And they still walk
through the trails
by the river

And they read all

their favorite books
in the reading nook
he built where the crystal
sun-catcher she found
at a flea market flecks
a kaleidoscope of
brilliant colors
onto the walls.

And sure they fight.
But neither one of them
fights to be 'right.'
And when things
got a little too heavy;
they'd forgive each other
for the night
and she'd make

coffee and cinnamon
rolls in the morning
where they'd set down
at the table and talk
until
they'd righted all that
they felt was wrong.

And though time had
worked its magic on
their hair and skin,

though they had old
creaky bones,
in their hearts they were
still young.

And if you asked either one
how they managed a
love for this long
they'd just smile and nod.
Neither loved each other
"the same as the day one"
but forever- more.
Everyday, more and more.